The Stories That Bind Us

BRIAN DUNNE et al

CONTENTS

37 Vida & Marta

38 Saleha & Fatima

39 Sacina & Rawda

40 Godfrey & Chloe

41 Ruta & Sofia

42 Marykutty & Evelyn

43 Anna & Blanka

44 Mary & Halle

45 Sheila & Erin

46 Sandra & Aishling

47 Margaret & Lauren

48 Olive & Áine

49 Attracta & Kyra

50 Teresa, Mick & Mia

51 Noel & Olivia

52 Sarah, Stephen & Sophie

53 Jayne & Rose

54 Michelle & Ella

55 Jennifer & Zara

56 Lisa & Saoirse

57 Anthony & Laila

58 Pat, Nicola & Ali

59 Waffaa, Ahmed & Sarah

60 Emma & Mia

61 Jaki & Mia

62 Luca & her Mom

63 Danielle & her Grandmother

64 Valentina & her Mum

65 Emma & her Dad

66 Leah & her Grandad

67 Hanna & her Grandparents

68 Alexandra & Aelys

69 Sienna & her Grandfather

70 Caoimhe & her Mom

71 Andras & Izidora

72 Kayleigh & her Nan

73 Madison & her Nan

74 Jency & Jewel

75 Orla & her Mum

76 Kayla & her Dad

ACKNOWLEDGEMENTS

This book was produced due to the efforts of a core group of VMware Ireland employees who joined together to partake in Age Actions Big Corporate Challenge which is a six-month Corporate Social Responsibility (CSR) program to encourage corporate teams to promote intergenerational connection while raising funds and awareness to support Age Action's work. All profits from this book go to Age Action.

This book would not be possible without the work of the following people. Thanks to you all for your efforts.

Jamie Knoblauch

Shane O'Connor

Eliee Fitzgerald Garcia

Tim Daniel

Brian Dunne

Final thanks to all the students from Scoil Mhuire in Ballincollig whose students contributed all of the stories and pictures in this book.

FOREWARD

"There are only two lasting bequests we can give our children - one is roots, and the other, wings." — Hodding S. Carter

The book you hold in your hands is a beautiful example of the legacies we leave to our children. Stories about family, whether they be silly, serious, or profound, have the power to both ground children in their family roots and give them a sense of what's possible to achieve in a lifetime. But for us at Age Action, what's more important than the stories themselves is the way we collect them.

Over the past year, we have seen how prevalent ageism is in our society. Ageism refers to how we think, feel, and act toward other people on the basis of their age. Throughout the COVID-19 pandemic, we have seen the ways that older people are depicted as vulnerable, frail and lacking agency. At the same time, we have seen younger people being depicted as irresponsible in public discourse and on social media. , The past year affirmed to Age Action how important it is to foster deeper understanding between generations, now more than ever. That's where this book comes in.

Collecting stories from their older family members, children have had a chance to hear about the experiences of their family members throughout their lifetimes. We can see from the stories and illustrations how authors were able to build each story into their own sense of family history, and perhaps even to their sense of self.

At Age Action, we believe that intergenerational connection is one of the most powerful tools for combatting ageism. By having people of all ages increase their contact with and respect for other generations, we can work together to build a society that values us as we grow older. The proceeds from the sale of this book all go directly to Age Action to support our work advocating for equality and human rights as well as our services: Getting Started digital literacy tutoring, our Care and Repair DIY home repair programme, and our Information Service.

Thank you to the independent team at VMware who put together this book, the pupils of Scoil Mhuire school in Ballincollig who contributed, and to those of you who purchased the book as well. By purchasing this book and supporting Age Action, you are helping to build a better world – not just for older people today, but for future generations.

Sincerely
Paddy Connolly (CEO Age Action)

1. ELEANOR, MARY & ELA

My great-grandmother Eleanor was born in Butte City, Montana in America. When she was five years old, she came to Ireland with her parents because her uncle had died suddenly. They had to help her nanna take care of the farm.

It took nine days to travel by boat from America to Bantry. The Princess Beara boat brought them to Castletownbere, where a neighbour was waiting with a pony and trap to bring them home. They brought one large trunk with all of their belongings in it.

The trunk is still in the farmhouse in Castletownbere where I often visit.

Nana Mary shared this story with Ela

2. MAURICE & BEA

My grandfather grew up in Glenahue in Kerry. Behind his house there is a glacial valley called "Maca na Bó". He has told me the story of the "Screecher" of Maca na Bó.

According to the people who lived in the valley the Screecher was an otherworldly spirit that emitted a gut-wrenching wail in the valley like the screech of a goat.

People said the Screecher looked like a black dog or sometimes took the form of a barrel. Some people felt the barrel was rolling after them and as they walked faster the barrel would increase its speed. People would run home and bolt the door behind them before hearing the thud of the Screecher behind them as it struck the door. Then it disappeared.

Legend has it the Screecher never crossed the river to the Eastern side of the valley.

Eventually everybody moved to the safer side.

Maurice shared this story with Bea

3. MAGDY & SARAH

Israel took a part of Sinai for a period of time and refused to give it back to Egypt. They built a high sand wall called the Bar Lev Line to prevent the Egyptians going in. The Egyptian army devised a plan to get ready for war, to get back the Egyptian land in Sinai.

One of the Egyptian army leaders had the idea to knock down the Bar Lev Line with water hoses. They chose the 10th of Ramadan while most of the soldiers were fasting. They chose 2:00pm where the sun is perpendicular on the desert and really hot so that the enemies would not predict the attack. They succeeded and got our land back. Every year Egypt celebrates the sixth of October in remembrance of the war.

My grandad was a leader in the Egyptian army. He was in the fight too. The war was in 1973.

Magdy shared this story with Sarah

4. KATE

My great grandparents long ago had servants.

All the women had to bake all the food by themselves. They had to milk the cows by hand, and they had no hot water, so they waited for it to rain and they had barrels outside to collect the rain. After it stopped raining, they would go out and collect the barrels and heat the water.

They also had to grow all their own vegetables.

Kate told this story

5. EUGENE & EMILY

My grandpa's best friend's mom had a dream that God gave her, like, a little peek into the future.

It was, like, an accident on the road.

So, she called her son and said not to drive on the road for a little while and then he said "Okay" but my grandpa was already on the road to Dublin.

He was really tired, and he fell asleep while he was driving and hit a truck. He hit the steering wheel and broke a rib. The rib went into his heart and he died.

He was on the news.

My dad was only 9 when this happened.

Eugene shared this story with Emily

6. WENDY & LAURA

When my great grandad was 10 years old World War 2 happened and Russia and Germany attacked Poland and Britain.

So, my great grandad was sent away to the stables to work with his younger brother who was 8 at the time.

Their mom was sent to work at camps.

The war went on for years, but my grandad was lucky because he only had to work for some of the time. Then when Britain helped Poland, they teamed up and won – hurray!

When Germany and Russia lost, they zoomed out and it was like the lottery. Everyone got to pick a free house and that house that my great-great-granny chose was the one that my mom grew up in and my nana is still living in it.

Wendy shared this story with Laura

7. DANNY & ROBYN

I remember my dad told me about this old man he helps because he is a health worker, so he helps people with disabilities.

The man lived for 96 years and he was in World War 2 and he was 18 and he was dropping bombs from the plane. He did not want to, but he had no choice.

Danny shared this story with Robyn

8.THERESA & TABITHA

When my grandma's mom was 10 World War 2 started and she needed to be evacuated from her hometown to a safer part of England with her brother and sisters.

They were packing a lot of stuff, so much that they missed the boat!

This boat had a lot of her class on it, and she felt a bit sad. A day went by and my great grandma got the news that the boat was bombed by the Germans and everybody on that boat sadly died.

She was very upset but glad that she was late to that boat.

Theresa shared this story with Tabitha

9. PALMIRA & MAFALDA

Once upon a time in a village called Malhadancha, in Castelo Branco in Portugal, there was a little girl aged 6.

In the 1940's the little girl, age of 6, is my great grandmother, she is great!

She did babysitting, even if she herself needed it! She was 6! Anyway, since she was small, she fell asleep while she was babysitting, like naps, and the baby would cry for long periods of time and as soon as the baby's parents found out she got hit and slapped and she was hurt.

She did in house babysitting and when the family were eating there was really good food in front of her but the family sent her to do chores or get wood so they would eat it all. When she came back there was nothing but bread and olives.

Plus, her dad took the money she earned.

My great grandmother is still alive! She is 86 now.

Palmira shared this story with Mafalda

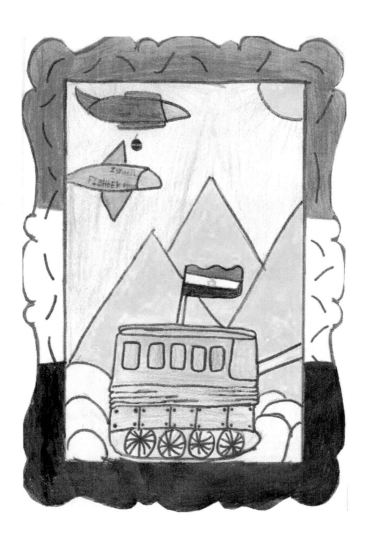

10. MOHY & KINDA

My grandfather's name is Mohy. He was in the war on the 6th October with Israel in year 1973. He was 30 years old.

The war ended in the same year. He worked in space rockets in the war. He was married to my beautiful grandmother who died 4 years ago. Luckily when my grandfather went to war he survived.

Now in Egypt we still celebrate the war and that we won. On the other side people still died.

Well, I am happy that my grandfather was alive and also that he was in the war. Now he is 78 years old, and I will always love him for what he did for Egypt.

I hope that you enjoyed my story.

Mohy shared this story with Kinda

11. ALICE & LUCY

My grandmother's mother would send her husband to collect nettles when it was nettle season.

In Spring her dad would collect as much as he could carry for that day and her mother would make nettle soup for tea/dinner.

They would eat it for health and after they would get the liquid from the lid and rub it on their wounds.

1bag of nettles would last them 1-2 days because they had 10 kids and 2 parents.

Alice shared this story with Lucy

12. TINA & MAOLÍOSA

When my mam was in infant school, she can remember small bottles of milk (1/3 of a pint) being given to all the children every day at morning break time. The milk was given free of charge by the dairy and was supported by the local council.

My mam also remembers as a child the milkman delivering bottles of milk on a milk float. Every morning on the front doorstep. The glass bottles over time were replaced with plastic and cardboards cartons.

A coastal village in Wales called Aberporth has reintroduced glass bottles in the last few years.

Tina shared this story with Maolíosa

13. CARLOS & ZENAIDA

When I called my granny she told me that my great grandad Carlos lived in a small town in Spain and sometimes they all went with a horse to a beach.They woke up very early and arrived very late.

Once they couldn't go in, so they went in the countryside where there were no houses. They were going to go on one path, but a woman told them to go the other way because there were shifting lands and they could get stuck, and they could die.

So, they were going to thank the woman, but she wasn't there. They went safely and they thought that the woman was the Virgin Mary because she could not have gone so quickly.

Carlos shared this story with Zenaida

14. MERCEDES & AIMEE

When my granny (my mum's mum) was younger...

One day my granny decided to get up early so she would be early for school. She got up, got dressed, brushed her teeth, ate breakfast and went out the door.

Her mum and dad were still asleep.

It was still dark outside, so she walked to school and the nuns saw her. There was a nun and my granny was her favourite student, so they asked why she was there so early and they invited her into the convent and they gave her tea, sweets and porridge.

Meanwhile the nuns rang her mom to tell her she was OK and an hour later people started coming.

My granny was the first in the convent.

Mercedes shared this story with Aimee

15. ANWITA

A story passed from my granny to my mom and from my mom onto me...

Once upon a time there was a king, who had three wives. One day a ceremony was coming. In the ceremony 1 king and 1 queen can sit. He asked his ministers what to do because he loved all three of them, but he needed to pick the wisest queen who can rule the kingdom. So, the ministers had a great plan.

The king called all three of his queens to announce his thoughts. The king asked his ministers to give a 1kg bag to each queen. The bag was full of grains. The king asked the queens to keep the bag safe until he asked for it back. All the queens took the bags and went.

After 1 year when the ceremony day was closer the king called the queens to get the bags to the assembly hall. All the queens came after the king's announcement.

He asked the first to give the rice bag. The king found the bag was fully rotten. The second queen gave the bag which was eaten by rodents. The third queen asked the king for one more hour. After the hour had passed two large trucks with 50 bags of rice each. "What is all of this?" said the king. "This all came from the bag of grains you gave me" the third queen said.

The king was impressed so he made her the queen of the kingdom. Anwita told this story

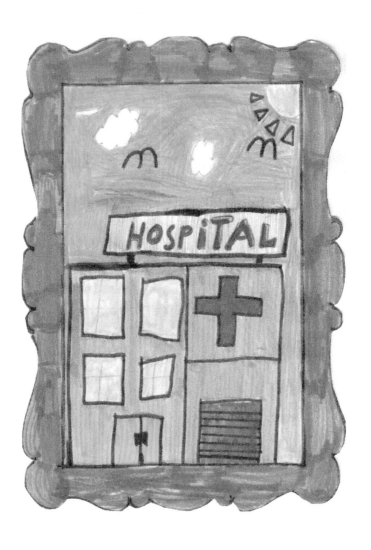

16. MALGORZATA & ZUZANNA

A long time ago, 1986 when my grandma was pregnant with my auntie and my uncle, the hospitals did not have the professional equipment they do now. So the nurses were so surprised when they found out she was going to have twins.

My great granny always used to tell her that this was very common in the family but she never believed her until that day.

Malgorzata shared this story with Zuzanna

17. ANDREA & DORKA

When my mom was on holiday in Croatia with her friends, she and two of her friends went on a ship to the city in Italy called Venice. Her and one of them got seasick so they decided not to take the ship back to Croatia.

They went to the railway station and got a train to Trieste. They arrived at evening and there was no bus or train back to Poreč, so they called their friends who were still in Poreč to come pick them up. They were stopped on the border though.

She found out there would be a bus to Poreč the next morning, so they went to find the bus station. They gave up and decided to call a taxi instead. They ended up near the railway station in the other direction!

So, they had to sleep outside the railway station with no blankets and no pillows.

Andrea shared this story with Dorka

18. VIKTORIJA

My great grandad was 15 when the war started.

The German soldiers took him and his younger brothers
to the labour camp. They had to work really hard and
didn't get enough food.

Many people wanted to escape from the labour camp.
Some of them tried and ran 2 kilometres from the camp
and hid in a stack of hay. The German soldiers looked for
them and found them. Nobody ever saw them again.

The rules were very strict. For anything you did wrong
they would get shot.

Viktorija told this story

19. ALISON & OLIVIA

When my granny was 8 she moved to England.

She went to school and was excited for her first day. Her teacher gave her roll-call number to her and of course, Murphy's law, being from Ireland her roll-call number was thirty-three but being from Ireland she pronounced it as 'tirty-tree'. So, she called out her number and everyone started laughing at her.

She ended up living there until she was 21, then she came back and she met my grandad.

This is a phrase my granny always says, "It's nice to be important, but it's more important to be nice!".

Alison shared this story with Olivia

20. PAT, KEVIN & GRÁINNE

My dad, Kevin, went camping with his dad, Pat, and three brothers in Killarney when he was 8.

It was raining all day, so they stayed in their tents.

Later on that night it stopped raining and they made a fire. There were thousands of midges flying around them. So, his dad covered him in a sleeping bag and put his arms around him to keep him from getting bitten.

The next morning there was not a bite on him, but his poor dad was covered from head to toe.

Kevin shared this story with Gráinne

21. KAROL & SOFIA

During World War 2 my grandad's family hid a Jew in their basement.

My family did not have much food but they still shared what they had.

The Jew never went out from the basement. Only sometimes during the night.

They saved his life.

Karol shared this story with Sofia

22. WIESTAURA & SARAH

When my great granny was little, there was war in Poland.

She was just about to start school when it started. When there was war no one went to school. When she was 13, she started first, she went to 3rd class but in the next few days moved up to 5th class. She only stayed in school 7 years then started work.

There were kids of different ages in one class, some were very young and others very old. Their school was too small for loads of classes. My grans school was an all-girls school as well but that was her secondary school.

They also wore uniforms back then and it was mandatory. If you weren't wearing your uniform, you got detention.

Wiestaura shared this story with Sarah

23. PHILIP & FREYA

My grandad's name is Philip.

When he was 10 he used to wake up at 6 o'clock in the morning. Then he had to walk up to the local newsagent and he collected a big heavy bag of newspapers. Then he walked down the street delivering them to each house. This is called a paper round. He went home and got ready for school. He would get paid 10 shillings (50c) per week. He could buy loads of sweets with that money.

He did this for three years. He delivered newspapers from Monday to Saturday in all weathers. When it was raining he had to be extra careful not to get the newspapers wet.

At Christmas he would knock on the doors and he would give them their newspaper and they would give him a tip. He would spend his tips on premium bonds which are a bit like lottery tickets. He had to deliver the newspapers even when he was sick.

My grandad grew up in Sheffield in Yorkshire in England.

Philip shared this story with Freya

24. JOHN & EVE

My grandad's name is John. He was born in 1935. He was born at home not at hospital. He is the oldest out of three and he's the only one still alive. He went to Blarney National School.

He went to work for the ESB and was involved in the building of the Iniscarra dam which brought electricity to homes in 1957. He went to England in 1959 to work and returned in 1971.

As a child he remembers playing around Blarney castle ground with his brothers and his friends. They used to play cowboys and Indians in and out of the castle.

He also remembers that his father worked for the Cork and Muskerry railway which closed in 1934 but his father continued to work for the railway line. He left school at an early age and had many jobs during his lifetime. He was 12 when he got his first job and he continued to work until the age of 79!

He has had his 2 vaccinations against Covid 19 and he's feeling great! He had 9 grandchildren, ages go from 3 to 31 years old.

John shared this story with Eve

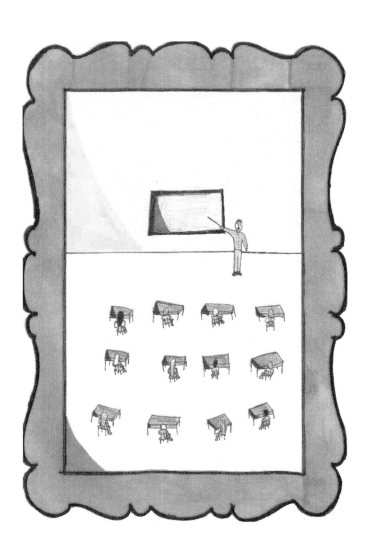

25. BARBARA & VERONICA

Back in the days, my mom went to school from 1980-1988. My mom lived 3km away from her school. When she woke up she got dressed into her blue dress uniform, made her lunch, ate her breakfast and cycled to school.

Surprisingly there were radiators back in those years. There were about 30 pupils in her class. For three years my mom had the same teacher (1st – 3rd class). Then from 4th to 8th class she had different teachers for different subjects.

In Poland there was 1st – 8th class, unlike Ireland in my school we have junior infants to 6th class. They got homework everyday even Friday. For Friday homework they had to read lectures for Monday.

At the end of the year they got reports, the scores went from not good to excellent. At the start of the year all the classes would line up in a square, the principal would stand up in the free spot.

The girls would wear a granite dress with a white collar, boys would wear a granite shirt and pants with a white collar.

At the end of the year this would happen too, the principal would give the people with the highest score a red ribbon with some writing on it.

Barbara shared this story with Veronica

26. MARTIN & JENNA

When my granda was younger, he and his best friend Drew found an axe in his shed. They were just after seeing the movie Vikings so they started to play with it.

They had to throw it behind them and see who could throw it the furthest. My granda threw it far so Drew wanted to as well. My granda's friend told my granda's youngest brother, Gary, to step back so he wouldn't get hit but Drew swang the axe into his head.

He had to go to hospital to get stitches. Drew thought he would get into trouble so he ran home and my granda never saw him again.

Martin shared this story with Jenna

27. ORLA & EMMY

One day my nana and her siblings went into a blackberry field to go pick blackberries. Meanwhile when they were picking, a wild bull came along! They ran for their lives!

Their fingers were purple and they felt sick because they were after eating so many berries. They entered the next blackberry field. They filled up their baskets and started to walk home.

My nana needed help from her older siblings to run away from the bull!

Their mother made blackberry jam. All of them thought it was worth all of the trouble of finding the berries.

They put the jam on everything, even on toast!

Orla shared this story with Emmy

28. CYNTHIA & CHANTELLE

When my mother was about 12 her family were very poor.
She had eight siblings, six sisters and two brothers. Their
dad left at a very young age.

There were seven girls in my mom's family but sadly one
of her sisters passed away. My grandmother was too poor
to take her to the hospital. Her name was Uba in
Nigerian, in English it means Light.

When my mom was older people bullied her for the way
she looked but my mom's sisters would always stand up
for her. When my mom was sixteen she got a job. She
sold food at a stand. She saved the money and she worked
for three years so she could move to Ireland to get a better
job and that's what happened.

When she turned 20 she said her goodbyes, took he bags
and then she was on her way to Ireland!

Cynthia shared this story with Chantelle

29. ESTER & ABIGAEL

When my grandma was young she lived in the country with her grandma and grandad. They had a tea house and racing cyclists used to call every weekend. They brought energy stuff to eat. They always gave her some and it tasted delicious.

Her grandma used to have an open fire in her house. She used to have a nice warm area. She used to hang an iron pot over the fire. In the iron pot she baked cakes on the lid of the pot she baked potatoes.

Travellers used to make copper pots and sell them to her. They ate the potatoes which were covered with butter and on the side they drank butter milk.

She also made delicious rice in a double pot on the stove.

This story took place in the late 50's or the early 60's.

Ester shared this story with Abigael

30. SHEHLA & HADIAH

One day when my mum was small, she went to Abu Dhabi with her family as her dad worked there. Her mother told her to go to the shop and buy evaporated milk to make tea. She gave her some money and off went my mother to the shop. When she reached there, she bought four to five evaporated milk tins. At that time, the tins were smaller than today's.

So then the shopkeeper gave her a bag to carry the tins with. She put the tins in the bag and headed off for home. On her way, she didn't notice that there was a hole in the bag and she kept going. At each place she passed by a tin fell out. When she reached home the last tin fell out and hit the doorstep. "Oh, what was that sound", she said. She looked down to see the tin rolling on the ground and nothing but a hole in her bag. She retraced her steps and picked up the tins. When she picked up the last tin she saw the shop again.

She went in and told the shopkeeper what happened. She asked for a new bag too. The shopkeeper said sorry for giving her a broken bag by accident. She said it was ok and took the tins home.

She told the story to her family and they laughed at her, and she found it funny too.

Shehla shared this story with Hadiah

31. VLADIMIR, JUTJANNA & KIRA

When my grandpa was younger he lived in an area of Russia with active volcanos.

One of his family members was part of the army.

When my grandma was younger and still in school she would walk to school and she had one uniform which was grey.

When she was in 6th class her grandma made her a dress for special occasions.

Vladimir & Jutjanna shared this story with Kira

32. LANA & KATE

I am going to tell you about my mam's busy Summer holidays in Latvia when she was a child.

There were really no proper days to relax. There were always chores to do. She had to help her mother gardening – picking weeds, planting seeds and watering plants. There were days to go to the woods to pick berries like blueberries, wildberries, raspberries, cranberries and blackberries. She also picked mushrooms too. There was enough for the whole winter to get natural vitamins for the whole family.

Another responsibility was to scrape the hay for her grandmother's cows. It was a really hard job.

There were also chores from the school. During the summer for one week, she had to do different jobs around the school – painting, cleaning paths, picking weeds from football pitches and some other jobs. At the same time she had to pick certain amounts of different herbs and to bring them to the pharmacy to sell for herbal teas.

That was my mam's summer holiday every year. It wasn't really fun but made her strong.

Lana shared this story with Kate

33. CLAUDE & LIZ-MAY

My grandma's name is Claude, she is 73.

When she was a child she went to her grandma's house for every holiday. She was living near the French mountains called Les Alpes.

Her grandma's job was to clean people's laundry. But there was no washing machine, so she had to go to the fountain to wash the laundry. The water of the fountain was coming from the mountains.

The symbol of this town is my grandma's grandma's house. If you go there and buy a souvenir the house will be on it.

Claude shared this story with Liz-May

34. DAN & EMMA

My grandad's name is Dan.

When he was a child he used to go to school, but in school there was no electricity, so they used to use oil lights, which are lights that use oil as fuel and they also used candles too.

He used to walk 3km to school and 3km back home again with all of his friends. They used to have great fun.

He used to do his homework on the kitchen table. The light was not good, especially in the winter. He used to do it under an oil light.

When electricity came it was amazing. That was in 1950 in my grandad's village and my grandad was ten years old (the same age as me).

Dan shared this story with Emma

35. CHRISTY & FAYE

When my grandad was just ten years old and they lived in a small two-bedroomed house with the toilet outside in a shed.

They played football every day in the square and every now and then the police would come and chase them all. One day, my grandfather got caught by one of the police, whom they nicknamed "Buckeye Fin". He had to go to court and was fine 2 and 6 pence by the judge.

Of course, his dad was not happy with him. He had learned his lesson, so he never got caught again.

Christy shared this story with Faye

36. CELIA & EVIE

My grandma used to live on a pig farm with 600 pigs. My great grandad used to own the farm.

They used to breed pigs and if they thought the pigs weren't going to breed, they would bring the pig into a special place and sit watching the pigs just in case.

When the piglets were sick, they would go to the bottom of the farmhouse and put the piglets into a haybarn so they wouldn't be cold or sick anymore and take them back to their mum.

When the piglets were a bit older, they would move them into a bigger building. They called it shifting the pigs.

Sometimes they would muck out the pigs.

Celia shared this story with Evie

37. VIDA & MARTA

It was a cold winters day. My granny had just got a new pair of beautiful knitted gloves.

One day, she decided to wear them for the first time to school. After school, she and some of her friends went together to jump on haystacks. But when she was going home, she found out that she had lost one of her brand-new gloves!

She didn't tell anyone that she lost it because she thought that her granny would be very mad at her if she told her. So, she went out with only one glove while the other hand was cold. So she kept that hand in her pocket.

But one day in the warmer springtime, she went to the same place with the haystacks and suddenly found the missing glove.

Vida shared this story with Marta

38. SALEHA & FATIMA

When my mommy was 6 or 7 years old, she lived in a city while her grandad lived in a village.

One day her dad had to do some work in the village, so my mommy stayed there for 10 days! She said it was really fun and an enjoyable experience. It was fun for her to sleep outside under the stars and wake up to a beautiful morning! It went very well!

And if you're wondering what she did, well it was very surprising for her that as a child, she had the freedom to play all around the village! She used to go to fields of corn and small hills. She found different types of plants and saw the farmers working with bulls and buffalos in the fields! And sheep grazing around.

It was an amazing memory of her childhood.

Saleha shared this story with Fatima

39. SACINA & RAWDA

My granny's name is Sacina. It means feeling safe and comfortable. She was born in 1949.

She started primary school when she was 6 years in 1955. Every table was for two children, the teacher wrote on a blackboard. There was electricity but it was weak and not available all the time.

When she finished primary school her mother and grandmother died at the same time from an electricity accident. Then she looked after her siblings with her father.

She worked as a nurse.

She had four children, the eldest is my father. She died in 2019 on the 10th of December of lung issues.

Sacina shared this story with Rawda

40. GODFREY & CHLOE

My dad went on an adventure trip for two years and travelled to India. He arrived in Mumbai first and found that India is a nice, warm and welcoming place. Everyone in India appeared happy and content.

My dad noticed there are two social classes of people, but both appeared happy. He found it very interesting that the less privileged were more welcoming to tourists and visitors.

My dad visited so many places including well known places such as Jaipur also known as "Pink City". Pink City is famous for having a palace. The palace is called "Hawa Mahal" which means "The Palace of Winds". It has 953 small windows.

He also visited the Taj Mahal. My dad was taken for a tour around the palace he saw where the king and queen were laid to rest. The most interesting part of visiting the Taj Mahal was that my father learnt all the workers who helped build the Taj Mahal had their hands cut off. This was ordered by the king because he did not want the Taj Mahal to be built anywhere else in the world.

My dad really enjoyed travelling around India. He loved their food and the smell of all the spices. The people were so nice and welcoming and my dad hopes one day he will return to India to visit those places again with his family.

He will never forget his time in India.

41. RUTA & SOFIA

My mom, when she was little, always loved her pacifier.
She just couldn't get rid of it.

One day, she got this big, yellow bear. She always put her
pacifier under his bum. She was four at the time.

One day, her dad got so fed up, he took the pacifiers and
hid them. When my mom woke up, she asked "Where are
my pacifiers?". Then her dad said, "The bear ate them!".
She picked the bear up, took him to the toilet and sat him
down on the potty. She started to shake her finger at him
and said, "Ok, listen up bear, poop them out!".

Ruta shared this story with Sofia

42. MARYKUTTY & EVELYN

My grandma's name is Marykutty but people who can't pronounce it call her Mary. My grandpa prefers to call her Mary.

My grandma is the oldest in the family of eight children. She has four sisters and three brothers. She was born on the 30th January, 1951. She used the light form the candle in school and at home for learning and other stuff. My grandma got electricity when she was 25.

She loved to play 'Sat' with her brothers and her sisters and also with her school friends. Sat is the name we use for "Dip The Can". We still call it Sat instead of Dip The Can.

My grandma has two children, a boy and a girl. The boy is the youngest and the girl is the oldest. The boy is my father. He has two children, one is me and the other is my baby brother. The girl is my auntie and she is in the USA and she has five children. Three girls and two boys. The boys are twins.

I love my grandma.

Marykutty shared this story with Evelyn

43. ANNA & BLANKA

When my granny was about 6 years old, she decided to prepare a special breakfast for her mum (my great-granny) for Mother's Day. She decided to make scrambled eggs.

She hadn't cooked anything before, but she watched her mum doing scrambled eggs for her and she really liked it.

In the morning, she went quietly to the kitchen and took out some eggs and fried them in the frying pan. She was very pleased with herself. When the eggs were ready, my granny gave them to her mum and wished her a happy Mother's Day!

My great granny was very happy and surprised that my granny cooked her breakfast. She had a taste of it and made a strange face. She put her plate away and hugged and kissed my granny. Then my granny asked her if they are so good why don't you finish? Then my great granny ate it all and complimented my granny again.

Then years later my great granny admitted that the eggs were burned very hard without any butter and very salty, but she could see that my granny tried so to make them.

So, for her, this was the best breakfast ever!

Anna shared this story with Blanka

44. MARY & HALLE

When my nana was younger, she had to walk a mile to the school bus. Her school was very new, it had pupils of various different age groups. She was very lucky to have all three of hre brothers in her class. Sadly, her school had to close due to a lack of pupils. And in the morning, she would bring her milk and tea in a bottle and keep it near the fire, and it would be hot for lunch time.

After school, my nana used to do a lot of playing outside because she did not have phones or iPad. She used to get a string and a conker and make a hole in it with anything she could get her hands on.

In her spare time, she would collect tadpoles and feed them weeds. By the way, she stored them in a jar.

She later grew fond of a doll who she would later go on to name Lily. She used to make daisy chains and necklaces. In school she had one teacher but thankfully in secondary school there was a few teachers.

Now she is 60 years old and has three children and two grandchildren.

Mary shared this story with Halle

45. SHEILA & ERIN

When my nana was seven or eight years old, she had 8 other brothers and sisters and lived in a house with no water or electricity.

Every day they took turns going to the well in a nearby field to get water. They needed the water for cooking, washing themselves and their clothes. One of them would have to go a few times a day to get water.

The well over the Summer would be dry so my nana and her eight brothers and sisters would have to walk an extra field down to get water from a farmer's tank. Luckily the farmer didn't mind.

Sheila shared this story with Erin

46. SANDRA & AISHLING

A few years ago, when my mom was working in Moscow, she got to the metro station early in the morning to go to work. She then realised that the clocks had changed the night before and that it was now really early in the morning and when she got on the train she dozed off.

She woke up suddenly and realised she had just missed the announcement telling people to get off and change trains. There were no people there and the train was moving along into a dark and deep tunnel. There was nothing my mom could do!

She was wondering how this would end. Was this train going to be parked for the weekend? Eventually the train arrived into an area where there were other trains and platforms and the doors slammed back and when she looked out of the train it was really high over the platform and she couldn't get out.

She spotted two guys and called them. They started laughing at her and told her to stay on the train as it would be going back shortly and not to worry.

My mum had, by then, missed the fast-connecting bus to her work. She had to get the one that makes all the stops so instead of arriving early she arrived late.

Sandra shared this story with Aishling

47. MARGARET & LAUREN

One day when my mom was in 1st class she came home from school. She wanted to play doctors with her sister so she did.

Her sister was the patient, and my mom was the doctor. So my mom's sister went to the room where the doctor was. She sat down on the chair waiting for the doctor to give her the right medicine (in the game).

When my mom gave her the medicine (a single block of lego) but my mom's sister actually ate it!

She had to go to the real hospital and get a real x-ray. They saw the piece of lego in her and they were able to get it out.

She was okay after all that.

Margaret shared this story with Lauren

48. OLIVE & ÁINE

When my mom was a child, my granny only let them have a treat on Friday so my mom and uncle got jelly cubes and hot water so that they could make jelly. They brought the hot water and jelly cubes into the sitting room and hid behind the couch. In the sitting room there was a cream carpet and when they were trying to make jelly some of it spilt onto the cream carpet!

When my mom was a child, her best friend lived up the road. One day my granny was outside putting up the washing. My mom got the cable phone and called her friend's house. Her friend's mom picked it up and shouted at my mom's friend that my mom was on the phone. Since my granny was outside, she could hear my mom's friend's mom, so she dropped the laundry on the table and marched into the house!

Olive shared these stories with Áine

49. ATTRACTA & KYRA

It was a hot Summer's day. We were looking forward to going to the river to paddle our feet.

But then our dad called us, and then we said Oh No!!! We knew what he was going to say. He was sending us to the mountain to do the turf.

We went in home and got our sandwiches and our wellies.

Along the way we got gooseberries. We sat down and ate some. After a while we arrived at the mountain and started the turf. It was very hard work because we worked under the hot sun.

At 5 o'clock we finished and made our way home. When we got home dad said, "Did you do all the turf?" and we said yes.

The next day dad came home and looked very cross. He said you did someone else's turf!

Attracta shared this story with Kyra

50. TERESA, MICK & MIA

In 2018 my nan and grandad (Teresa and Mick) took me to Dublin to see Disney On Ice.

We got some food, and we got the Luas and I saw two little girls and I said hi and then we went to watch the show.

The food there was amazing then Mickey and Minnie announced that princesses were going to be there. There was Else, Anna, Belle and Cinderella.

I had a Minnie Mouse lifesaver!

We got the Luas home and we took the train.

Mia told this story

51. NOEL & OLIVIA

The year was 1953. On my grandad's first day of school his mother dropped him to school. He was playing in the sandpit when his mother suddenly left his sight. He wandered off home and his mom brought him back to school, but it kept on happening for a couple of days.

The year was 1956. When it was my grandad's communion day he went to the church with his family. When my grandad came home from the church, he went out playing football and he was still in his communion clothes. He ran on to the road and he got knocked down by a bicycle and his communion clothes got ripped. My grandad did not get into trouble because it was his communion day and his mom had to sew his communion clothes.

Noel shared these stories with Olivia

52. SARAH, STEPHEN & SOPHIE

When my mom was 7, she came second in an All-Ireland gymnastics competition.

My mom broke her leg when she was 8 or 9. She and her brother were on their skates and her brother told her to go in front of him so he wouldn't fall. Then he fell on top of my mom and she fractured her leg in two places. She had to wear a cast up to her hip.

Sarah & Stephen shared this story with Sophie

53. JAYNE & ROSE

When my mom was four years old, she went shopping with her mom. Without anyone in the store noticing, she would eat some jellies and they were not for free!

When her mom found out she got so mad and had to apologise to the shopkeeper.

Jayne shared this story with Rose

54. MICHELLE & ELLA

My mom went crab fishing nearly everyday when she was younger. Her sister, Pearl, would go with her after school to catch crabs.

They would catch loads of crabs but would never bring them home. Instead, they would put them back in the river.

Michelle shared this story with Ella

55. JENNIFER & ZARA

When my mom was 12 she walked over 6 kilometres to the "Beat on the Street" party with her friends but her mom didn't go. Red FM organised it and a band were playing on the street. It was organised at town. Over 1,000 people were there. There were loads of cars driving along the road playing loud music. She told me her mom made her a dress with old clothing and string. She knitted it. My mom didn't really like the dress, but she appreciated it. That night she wore the dress her mom was happy.

In the Summer my mom played a game of rounders and of course my mom's friends joined in. Rounders is a game where you throw a ball, and it lands in a net and then you run.

Sometimes my mom used to jump in a fountain!

When my mom was 9, she was riding her bike but got her leg stuck in the peddle. My mom had to go to the doctor, and she was in hospital for a few weeks. My mom's mom was very scared for her and her dad was very scared as well. She wore a special cast.

Jennifer shared this story with Zara

56. LISA & SAOIRSE

One day my mom was at home with her mom, her dad and her two brothers and two sisters. She was in the sitting room and was messing on her chair.

Suddenly she fell into the fire that she was sitting next to. She was six years old. She had to go to hospital but luckily, she had no scars.

Lisa shared this story with Saoirse

57. ANTHONY & LAILA

When my dad's brother was a teenager, he was drunk the day before Mother's Day. On his way back home, he went into someone's garden and took all of their flowers from their garden. When he got home, he put the flowers on the table with a card but never cut the roots off. The next day he said he bought them but my dad's mom knew he didn't buy them, and he got in big trouble.

When my dad was younger in school the teacher would whack the students with a belt when they were bold. There was a boy called Gerard and he kept on moving his hand back. Once he moved his hand back very quickly and the teacher whacked himself so hard that he nearly cried.

Anthony shared these stories with Laila

58. PAT, NICOLA & ALI

My dad was surveying fields across the country with his dad, Pat. They were checking routes for pipelines.

In one of the fields there were loads of young teenage bulls. My dad got chased by about fifteen of them and he had to run and jump over the field gate and onto the road.

When my mom was 11 or 12, she was walking to the library. At the pedestrian crossing at the Oriel, a car broke the red light and knocked her down.

She was taken by an ambulance to the CUH (Cork University Hospital). She spent three hours getting x-rayed.

She was totally fine, but she has a scar over her eye.

Pat and Nicola shared these stories with Ali

59. WAFFAA, AHMED & SARAH

One day my dad was playing outside when his mom called him. She said to get some bread. My dad didn't want to, as it was way too far. He had to walk for almost an hour. Eventually he got there and got the bread.

One day my mom was at home with her mom. My mom's mom told her not to use a knife, but my mom didn't listen and used it anyway. She used it, then she cut a tiny bit of her thumb and it was really deep. She had to get stitches in the hospital to close the cut.

Waffaa and Ahmed shared these stories with Sarah

flying to Ireland

60. EMMA & MIA

When my mum was ten on February the 14th she moved to Ireland from England.

She had to put all of her stuff in the car and there was no room left. She even had to bring her cat which had the most room out of all of the people in the car.

On March the 17th she moved to her new house and joined her new school.

She started in Scoil Mhuire in 4th class which is the same school I am in today!

Emma shared this story with Mia

61. JAKI & MIA

When my mom was seven, her sister, Anne, asked her did she want a backer on her bike.

My mom jumped on and her sister started cycling. My mom fell off the bike and hit her nose on the kerb.

She had to go to the hospital. My mom's nose and two fingers were broken. My mom had to have an operation to fix her nose and had a cast on her nose for six weeks.

She said it was very sore.

Jaki shared this story with Mia

62. LUCA & HER MOM

The Day My Grandad Brought Gummy Bears.

When my mom was small, she got a baby sister. She thought she could play anything she wanted with her. She realised that she was too small to play the games she wanted to play, she was a bit mad.

Then her grandad came to visit them from another country, and he brought them gummy bears as a gift. They were very excited because they had never had gummy bears before.

My mom was delighted because she thought that her baby sister would be able to eat the gummy bears. She tried to give her some gummy bears. She put lots of them in her mouth, but she did not eat them. My mom was very confused and mad because she could not understand why her baby sister did not like the gummy bears.

It turned out that her baby sister did not have any teeth yet and could not chew gummy bears.

Luca's mom shared this story with her

63. DANIELLE & HER GRANDMOTHER

Games My Grandmother Played.

My grandmother told me a story from long ago, of the games they used to play and the sweets she used to eat.

She would play "hop-scotch" and "piggy". She would play marbles. They would play skipping and chasing. They also would go to the park and play on the swings and slides.

Her favourite ice-lolly was called "Patsy-Pop" and her favourite crisps were called "Perri". They would also eat "bruss" which was a mixture of sweets and crumbs. They ate this from a cone made from newspaper.

I like listening to my grandmother when she tells me stories like this. I like these stories because they are different, and I learn new things about long ago.

Danielle's grandmother shared these stories with her

64. VALENTINA & HER MUM

The Scorpion.

When I was 7 years old, my house in Brazil had a lot of garden around it.

One day my granny came to pick me up to go to school. At the front of my house there was a scorpion and it stung me!

I had to go to the hospital and do a lot of tests and stayed the whole day. I felt very scared and worried. The next day I went to my nana's house. We all thought that the scorpion was dead. Suddenly the scorpion appeared in my nana's car. My nana screamed and was very scared. My nana was very brave and took the scorpion out of the car.

When I came back to school, I told the story because it was so unbelievable. My nana put the scorpion in a cup and brought it to school! All of my friends were amazed.

Valentina's mam shared this story with her

65. EMMA & HER DAD

The Day Dad Broke His Arm.

When my dad was 10 years old, he went to school in Adrigole, in the countryside. When it was break-time my dad decided to climb a wall. So that is what he did.

He started to swing like Tarzan. (It must have been really really high up there, otherwise he wouldn't have been able to break his arm.). He started to slip down. He fell all the way down and his left arm hit a big, hard rock. He could not move his arm, so he knew it was broken. It really, really, <u>really</u> hurt and he started to yelp in pain.

And worst of all, all of the mean rotten bullies laughed and picked on him (poor dad). But then again, the bullies didn't recognise how much pain he was in, did they? Then the teachers found out, called his parents, called the ambulance, then probably told the bullies off for laughing and picking on him.

Then, my dad had to go to Cork University Hospital to have two big operations on his left arm. One of the operations he had were probably for him to get fourteen stitches, at least, for his broken arm.

And yet, thirty-nine years later, he still has that scar with fourteen stitches on his left arm. It looks like this scar on that arm of his will never (even the slightest, teeniest, most microscopic amount you could imagine) never ever fade.

66. LEAH & HER GRANDAD

My Grandad Remembering the Moon Landing

It was 1969. I was having my holidays in Owenahincha. I was in the kitchen with my mother and my sister. We were in our bungalow holiday house.

We were listening to the radio to hear when they would take off. Neil Armstrong and Buzz Aldrin were going to the moon. I was so excited! 😊 They were leaving from a place in America called Cape Kennedy. Our transistor radio called "10, 9, 8, 7, 6, 5, 4, 3, 2, 1, blast-off!!!".

My sister and I were frightened. This was a dangerous part because this rocket could explode. But luckily it set off safely. So far, so good! Their rocket was called Apollo 11. First, the rocket had to orbit the Earth. The radio said where the rocket was and where it was going. A few days later, in the morning, the rocket landed safely on the moon. I was happy."

I think the story is interesting especially because they're on holiday like it's a special occasion (but it is, eh). I can't believe there was no Covid there because I can't remember normal life. I would have a big party if that happened to me. I am very happy about my story, I loved writing it too. YAY!

Leah's grandad shared this story with her

67. HANNA & HER GRANDPARENTS

How My Granny and Grandad Met

My granny worked in a candy factory. She made cotton-candy. She made lollies and all types of sweets.

One day a man came into the factory and saw my granny. The man was an employee. When he got stuck my granny went to help him. After three years they were married and working from home. They were making cotton-candy and bringing it to the factory.

Then my granny had my mom whose name was Petra. They loved her and four years later they had her sister. My granny and grandad lived a happy life with their two daughters. They lived in an apartment in the Czech Republic.

I really liked learning all about how my granny met my grandad. I love going to visit my granny and grandad because they always have interesting stories to tell me.

Hanna's grandparents shared this story with her

68. ALEXANDRA & AELYS

The Abandoned Dog

In 1990, my mum was playing with her friend and her brother. They were playing in a landfill. My mum saw five kennels and in one of the five kennels there was a boxer (not a boxer that boxes). It was a big, beautiful boxer. My mom and here brother and her friend opened the locker and the dog was running all around the landfill.

My mum, her friend and her brother brought it back to her house but her mum was not happy because they had another dog. It was an English Setter and the boxer kept running away back to the landfill.

Then the keepers of the landfill said to my mum that the dog was abandoned ,and they put him in the cage. So, my mum had to give the boxer to the pound. My mum was sad, but the landfill keepers said that the boxer found a very nice family.

My mum was very happy for the dog.

Alexandra shared this story with Aelys

69. SIENNA & HER GRANDFATHER

The Apple Orchard.

When my grandad was young, walking to school with 5 or 6 of his friends, they all went into an apple orchard. One of the boys would climb a tree to get some apples and throw them down to the rest of them. Then they would put them into their bags and would share them with their other friends in school.

But one morning, one of the friends went up in the tree to get more apples but then the owners of the orchard came out. They all ran and hid behind trees. But the other friend was still up the tree and couldn't get down. They had to wait for the friend to get down.

So, they were one hour late to school. They told the teacher that they were chased by cows as a lie. But their teacher found out what happened when the owners of the orchard came to the school and they got into a lot of trouble.

I like this story because it is funny and it's pretty different than now because most people wouldn't steal from orchards, they would buy them from the shops. And, it's funny when the boy got stuck up the tree.

Sienna's grandad shared this story with her

70. CAOIMHE & HER MOM

When My Mom Went to Trabolgan.

One Sunday afternoon, when my mom was four, she and her family went to Trabolgan. Her aunts and uncles came too. There were eight children. They had a great day. They went swimming, they played tennis and had a picnic.

At the end of the day, my mom and her family were playing hide and seek. It was almost home time, and the children were called to get in the car. Everyone was really excited because they were stopping for find and chips on the way home. There was one big problem… My mom didn't hear them call her back to the car and she was still hiding. A few minutes had passed when my mom poked her head out and saw that all the cars had gone. My mom got a fright. A member of staff asked my mom "Where are your parents?". My mom told her the story and she reassured my mom that they would come back.

There were no mobile phones back then so they couldn't phone her parents. Meanwhile, my nana and granda stopped for fish and chips in a nearby town and realised my mom was not in any of the cars. They quickly turned back and found my mom eating mints in the staff room and my mom still reminds my nana and granda to this day!

Caoimhe's mom shared this story with her

71. ANDRAS & IZIDORA

My great-great-great-grandfather was Hungarian who rode horses and was very good at it. Then his boss told him to go to Croatia. His girlfriend had to stay in Hungary. However, she was also having a baby, so she went to Croatia with him. And they lived with their three daughters in Croatia happily until the First World War began.

He was captured by the Russian Army and sent to Siberia. Then he tamed a horse and escaped. But the war was still on and he couldn't go home.

So, he rode the horse all the way east to the Pacific Ocean. Then he got on a ship all the way to North America, California. He travelled from California to Florida. Then he got on a ship, crossed the entire Atlantic Ocean, through the Gibraltar Strait into the Mediterranean Sea, to Greece, and from there back home to Croatia to his girlfriend and three daughters.

The entire trip lasted for fifteen years. The entire time he was writing letters to his girlfriend and daughters and mailing money he earned wherever he roamed. He always thought about them. And then they got married and lived happily ever after.

Andraš shared this story with Izidora

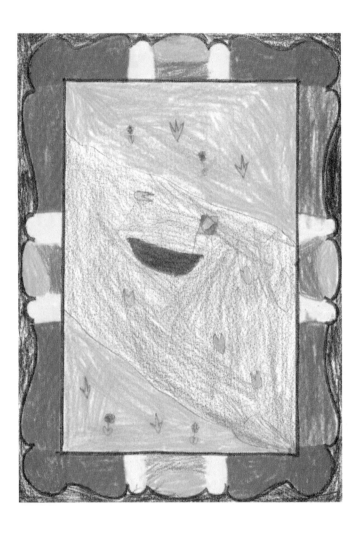

72. KAYLEIGH & HER NAN

How My Nan Grew Up

As a young child, my nan and her siblings used to walk to school every day. My nan lived and grew up in a house on the banks of the Lee in Inniscarra. They used to walk all the way from Inniscarra to Scoil Eoin which used to be a girl's school back then. For their lunch they used to have one sandwich they would have jam and butter. Every Sunday my nan and her family used to go to mass in St. Mary's and St. John's church. Her dad, my great grandad, used to own his own wooden row boat. On Sunday mornings, for mass, they all used to get into the row boat and cross the River Lee to the other side and walk the rest to get to the church. They used to have so much fun.

My nan said every Friday when her dad got paid, they used to walk to the shop and buy a jam cake and they all used to get a slice each. That was their treat for the week. They used to 'make and do' out of mud and sticks and play games with them.

My nan said I don't know how lucky I am with everything we have today.

There is so much I learned from my nan's story like, Scoil Eoin was a girl school, and everything was so different back then.

Kayleigh's nan shared this story with her

73. MADISON & HER NAN

My Mom's First Day in School

My mom's first day in school was over 25 years ago. My mom remembers being very scared and crying. She was nearly 5 in Junior Infants. Her teacher was Bean Uí Fuineachta. She remembers it was the first class next to the stairs. They had to say goodbye to their moms and dads which made them sad.

My mom can remember playing with marla, playdough, building blocks and stickle bricks. The principal was Bean Uí Aoidh and my mom remembers her being a very nice person.

I loved learning about my mom's first day of school. On my first day of school, I played with building blocks and playdough. We went out on the playground and had loads of fun. We don't play with marla, building blocks and stickle bricks.

My mom went to Scoil Mhuire, the same school as me. She didn't have a playground and the Corona virus didn't exist.

Madison's nan shared this story with her

74. JENCY & JEWEL

The Hare and The Turtle.

My mother's favourite story when she was young was "The Hare and The Turtle".

Long ago, there was an argument about who was faster. They decided to have a race. When they started the hare shot ahead for some time. He saw that he was far gone from the turtle. He was tired from running so he sat next to a tree and slept. When he woke up, he noticed that he had lost the race.

He asked the turtle for a re-match. The turtle said yes. This time the hare didn't stop running till he won the race.

Then the turtle asked for a re-match but this time a different route, the hare said yes. The hare ran ahead but he saw a lake. He stopped and was thinking about what to do. The turtle caught up and swam across the lake and won the race, leaving the hare stuck. The hare heard cheering and clapping in the distance.

Jency shared this story with Jewel

75. ORLA & HER MUM

A long time ago, in 1976, when my mum was 5 year old, she went to a school named "Saint Francis of Assisi's Primary School". Here are some subjects she did: maths, English, science, art, P.E., religion and history.

Art was one of her favourite subjects in school. She liked art because you can create anything you imagine, and that you can come up with any image in your head and that you can use anything you want to do it with, and that's why she loved art. She used all sorts of things like fairy liquid bottles, empty rolls of toilet paper, milk-bottle tops, sticks, yoghurt pots, coloured paper, card, cake liners, empty water bottles, straws, lollipop sticks and many more items!

She used to play games at school like skipping ropes, elastics, two tennis balls, tag, bulldog, hopscotch and kirby. People still play these games every single day. These games were very popular back then. The school wasn't far from her house, so she could walk there and back. Mum could take her bike to school, and even did her cycling proficiency test. Parents didn't drive children to school back then. Everyone walked even if it was raining or snowing. She had a school choir, she sang at masses for Lent, Christmas, Easter and Saint's days. There was also Brownies and Girl Guides. My mum was in both and became a young leader. She also did Irish dancing.

My mum misses her school a lot and would love to go back to those days.

76. KAYLA & HER DAD

The Life of my Grandmother.

My grandmother was born in the year 1954. She had her primary education in her village, Yebu North. She had joined her family and worked on their farm before she met my grandfather, then fell in love and got married.

After getting married they moved to Lagos, the old capital of Nigeria, where my father was born and his siblings. They had five kids and my dad is the second eldest. Four boys and a girl.

In 1996 tragedy struck when we lost my grandfather suddenly to a brief illness. Life then became difficult for my dad and his siblings, but my grandmother took it upon herself and filled the void left by my grandfather. She provided all their needs and gave them a good education.

And that's the end of my grandmother's story. She died long ago but she still has a pure heart

Kayla's dad shared this story with her

77. GRETTA & SOPHIE

Before I was born, my mum and dad lived in Auckland, New Zealand for a little while.

But before they got there they travelled around Thailand. My mum told me they got to ride an elephant and wash it in the river after. There are lots of lovely beaches in Thailand too. Bangkok is Thailand's capital city.

After Thailand they arrived in Auckland. They travelled all over the country and even got ot climb a glacier. They said New Zealand is very beautiful and a great country to live in.

I can't wait until I'm an adult so I can go travelling.

Gretta shared this story with Sophie

78. STEPHANIE, TOM & CIARA

In 1969 the TVs were all black and white. My granda remembers when he was small, he was staying up very late with his family because they were watching Neil Armstrong become the first person to set foot on the moon.

A few years later they got coloured TVs.

My nan remembers when she was young on the TV, she was watching the first woman president, Mary Robinson in 1990 and a few years later she met her in person. And then the second woman president, Mary McAleese, she met her in person as well.

Stephanie and Tom shared these stories with Ciara

79. PETER, ROBERT & HANNAH

A long time ago, my great-great-grandad Peter drove a big ship out on the sea. It was very dangerous because it was in the middle of the war.

So, they had to have protection, like steel boots or armour.

There was a big pit of boots, just left boots. He took out a boot and put it on his left foot and it fit. Then he put the left boot on his right foot, but it did not fit because it was a left boot. So, he cut the top off the boot and walked around with his toe sticking out.

I don't think he had much protection on his foot!

Dad Robert shared this story with Hannah

80. PAULA & SOPHIE

A long time ago, when my mom was my age, she came to this school.

When my mom was here there were no computers and there were no whiteboards. Now we have computers and there are whiteboards. The new building was not even here!

My mom wishes that all of that stuff was there. It was in the 1980's.

She thinks that I have loads of fun in school because of all these new things.

Paula shared this story with Sophie

81. SAYEEDA & MARYAM

My mom was born in Libya. After 2 years they moved to India. My granny was a teacher, and my grandad was a doctor, so they had to move a lot.

Then they went to Saudi. My mom went to school there. After some time, they went back to India.

When they went back to India, my mom stayed with her granny while her mom and dad went to Dubai, America and Ireland.

When her parents came back, my mom got married. After she had me, she had my sister.

Now we live here.

Sayeeda shared this story with Maryam

82. PETER & KINGA

My mom and dad lived in Poland. They went to school in Poland. My dad moved to Ireland in 2006. He worked in a bakery and he still does now.

When he was younger, he was running and hit his eye by the end of the door handle and now he has a red dot in his eye. He used to go to the woods with his friends and he liked to climb trees.

He had a dog that was kept in a cage. His dad had a horse. His dad let the horse for some runs around the field. One day, when the horse was on a run, the dog got out of its cage and the dog knocked the horse down.

I think it is very funny and I love to tell it.

Peter shared this story with Kinga

83. OLWIN & OLIVE

When my mum was younger, she went to Togher National Girls School. She lived across the road and walked with her sisters and cousins.

Every day at lunchtime at 1pm she was able to go home to have her lunch.

She was very happy there. Her favourite subjects were English and geography.

There were no whiteboards in her school, the teachers used chalk and blackboards.

I go to an all-girls school too, but it is very different.

Olwin shared this story with Olive

84. DERMOT, SINEAD & CLARA

When my mom was in 6th class in this school she got full marks. My principal was in Africa then. And she was my mom's teacher. Since she was in Africa and my mom got full marks, my principal got her two African combs. My mom was super happy! And we still have them.

My grandad went to school at the Community Hall. That was because Scoil Eoin was still being built. And now he writes the "History of Ballincollig". The "History of Ballincollig" is about the people who lived there and Ballincollig itself. He also went to school with my teacher's great uncle.

Dermot and Sinéad shared this story with Clara

85. BRIAN & EDITH

When my dad was young, he was on holiday with his family in Kerry. He was 6 years old.

My grandad told my dad and his brothers and sisters a story about a banshee. When my dad and his brothers and sisters went to bed, they got an awful fright.

The banshee from the story appeared outside the bedroom window.

After a few minutes, my dad's brother went to the window and pulled back the curtain. When he pulled back the curtain the banshee turned out to be my grandad with a tea towel on his head.

They all started laughing.

My dad still talks about it today.

I think it's funny because my dad got a fright.

Brian shared this story with Edith

86. BILLY & MANAL

When my mom went to boarding school in Africa, they had school on Saturday and Sunday. They were not allowed to go outside.

Some people had a job to give people lunch while others had to put the books in order.

At yard people had fresh air.

A few years later my mom graduated. She was so happy after she graduated.

My mom went to college and after that she met my dad!

Billy shared this story with Manal

87. JOHN & MIA ANNE

On the 12th of May 1974, my grandad went to Fermoy
because he wanted to join the army.

He was about 17 so he was allowed to join the army.

When he got there, he was disappointed because they were
not taking recruits at that time.

My grandad went back to the Cork City the following day.
My grandad decided he would join their army.

John shared this story with Mia Anne

88. FABIO & LAURA

A long time ago in the 1980's when my dad was still a child, he was playing around outside with his friends.

While they were playing, they came across something grey, as hard as a rock and big. It looked like metal. They thought that if it was metal and if they hit it, it would probably make a very loud noise. Then they found a strong stick.

"Let's hit it!", they said. My dad offered to hit it, so he did. It made a loud noise, so they kept on hitting it. To their surprise a bunch of bees flew out and stung them.

Now my dad says to never hit metal without knowing what's under it. He learned his lesson!

Fabio shared this story with Laura

89. LISA & BROOKE

My mom, when she was around my age, went to a convent school. She went to a convent school until she was 18. She did not like going there.

When she was around 17 or 18 my mom had a friend, who was the same age. One time, my mom's friend had enough of the nun. The nun was dragging her by the ear. The girl had enough, and she pulled her veil down. All of the nuns were very angry. The girl didn't care because the nuns were mean to her. My mom stayed out of it!

Also, my aunts were friends with her. They found out she moved to Mayo.

One day my mom was walking to school in the lashing rain. My mom came in late, and she got a belt on the back of the hand with a ruler, 7 times.

Lisa shared this story with Brooke

90. ISABELLA & HER GRAMPA

My mom's grampa loved horses.

He did horse-riding, races and the other racers called him "The Boss".

My mom and my granny were shown in the newspaper holding the trophy and he loved his dog.

Isabella's Mom shared this story with her

91. SHALINI & ANASHA

One sunny day, when my mom was little, she found a puppy in the streets.

She took it home and hid it from her parents. She hid it in the garden. She made a little home for the puppy and fed it.

Her parents didn't find out for two days, but my mom forgot to feed it.

Her dad found out and he said she can keep the puppy. My mom named it Puppy.

She would play with it everyday after school and she had so much fun.

Shalini shared this story with Anasha

Long Distance Phonecall

Shane's dad told him about a long distance phone call.
These days it is simple to pick up a phone and call
anywhere in the world using voice or video. Most of the
time there is not even a charge associated with this due to
the likes of WhatsApp and Facetime. It wasn't always that
simple. My dad shared this story with me...

On a Friday evening on coming home for the weekend I
called at my married sisters house as usual however that
weekend she was not home. My nieces informed me that
she was gone to my grandmother's home as she had just
died. I crossed the street and entered my father's family
home. Dad was one of 12 children, 4 boys and 8 girls all
but one married with families. All my uncles and five aunts
lived in Ireland, two aunts in England and one in Australia.

After extending my condolences to those gathered at that
time we were just chatting and settling in for a long night,
Uncle Sean announced that they had been able to contact
everyone except my aunt in Sydney Australia as she did not
have a telephone, he informed me that her next-door
neighbour had a phone but he did not know his name, that
was the problem. I said we should try to make contact,
they all agreed so Uncle Sean said to me that his office was
at the end of the hall and I could try and would not be
disturbed.

As it was about 1970 we still were using the wind-up
phone to ring the local exchange, Farranfore I think.
There was a very helpful receptionist there and I explained

my problem, my Grandmother had died and we were trying to contact all of her twelve children, there was just one outstanding, Auntie Norrie in Sydney, who did not have a phone. I did have an address though and I knew that her next-door neighbour had a phone. The receptionist did not hold much hope but she would try and would it be OK if she stayed listening to my progress, I said certainly and we started.

In no time I was talking to my aunt in Australia

She put me through to the exchange in Tralee where I had to repeat the story once again as was the case with the following exchanges, Dublin, Southampton England, New York, San Francisco, Hawaii and then Sydney Australia where it was mid-morning. Without a phone number or the name of the neighbour they decided they would ask the Police to help and this they did by supplying the name and telephone number of the neighbour so the Sydney exchange finally put me trough to Norrie's neighbour, I explained my reason for contacting him and asked if he could run next door and get Norrie which he did and in no time I was talking to my aunt in Australia. I just asked her to hold and I ran up the hall burst into the room where they were waking my grandmother and asked Sean and the other family members present to come quickly, they all did. I do not remember how long the call lasted but it was a long time as at least six of her immediate family spoke with her and her husband Tom.

When everything calmed down I said to Uncle Sean that I thought that would be the most expensive call ever made from that phone, he answered that it was worth every penny. I said it would be interesting to find out, he laughed and said the office is yours so I once again rang the local exchange got the same operator who said it was the most interesting night she ever had and there would be no

charge from her end and as she contacted each exchange
the answer was the same

NO CHARGE

The Sydney Police said they were only doing their duty.

93. SHANE O'CONNOR & HIS GAGA

The Eye Test

Shane's gaga has his eye test on the golf course
Gaga was an avid golfer and played well into his 80s. He
used to drive the 25km or so to Killarney Golf club two or
three times a week. He had a great circle of golfing
buddies, one of whom was his doctor.

One day when the two of them (Doc. G. & Gaga) were
playing Gaga teed off and drove the ball well down the
fairway (or so he says). He turned to Doc. G. and said,
Did you see where that went?

Doc. G. replied that he had not been able to follow the
ball. Gaga said, I saw it. My eyesight is fine! Here, sign
this. and handed him his eye-test report for his driver's
license. Of course, Doc. G. signed it

94. SHANE O'CONNOR & HIS GAGA

Young Daredevils

Shane's gaga and his friend were daredevils back in their youth

One time when Gaga was staying with us he asked me to bring him into the city to meet up with an old friend of his who he hadn't seen in many years. I said no problem and off we went. They were meeting up in a hotel that gaga's friend owned at the time. When we got there I made sure they met up and asked when he wanted to be collected, he said, "Sit down there, we won't be long."

After about four hours and many hilarious stories they said their farewells and we set out for home. I cannot remember all of the stories that were told but here is one of my favourites.

When gaga and Jack were in their early twenties (this would have been back in the early 1930's) they both saved up and each bought a motorbike. The motorbikes were their pride and joy and the two of them happily admit that they were like children with keys to the sweet shop. Like all red-blooded young men they wanted to see who had the best bike and also who was the best rider. They had a few races on the local roads but back then the condition of the roads was less than suitable for racing of any type, especially two would be Evil Knievals (a very famous American motorbike stunt rider) so they were unable to decide who would have been a winner.

However, these were two cute Kerrymen and something like bad roads were not going to stop them. They decided that if the roads would not work they'd have to find an alternative. One evening while socialising in a local pub they had the 'brainwave' (their words, not mine) to race along the railway. So a few days later they stripped the tyres off the two motorbikes and put one motorbike on each rail track. The wheel rims gripped the rail tracks and held them steady. So, the two of them got up on the motorbikes and had their races.

It's at this point that the stories branched out, each of them claiming that they had won the race. I suppose that after 60 years or so some of the details may have been lost. I did ask them how long the track had been unused for at that time and they said, "Oh, those tracks were still in use then, but we'd have seen any train coming"

95. SHANE O'CONNOR & HIS GAGA

Quick Quip

Shane's gaga had a great wit

In the last few months of Gaga's life, after he had a stroke, he was in an old folks home. They used to sit them all out together in this lovely sun-room. There was an elderly lady there and she was constantly talking - she would never shut up. Gaga asked one of the nurses to take her out the back and shoot her.

It's a Small World

Shane's cousin Jill shared this story about their grandfather

Gaga went to USA (chasing after a Castleisland girl, we won't mention names) not sure what happened with her...

He told me this story...

He was in the Kingdom house for a drink the night before he was heading and a second cousin of a second cousin came in and wrote the address of his brother who lived in New York on a beer mat or a scrape of paper. Gaga put it in in his back pocket.

He arrived at Ellis Island (just guessing that was where he arrived too) when you got to the port you had to show the address of the person you were staying with. Gaga's address was wrong it was missing a street name or something he was put into a room with 5 others with the same problem or maybe fake addresses (we won't go there).

"You're the spitting head of him" The secretary in the holding room kept on looking at him and then said "you have to be related to .... you're the spitting head of him". His cousin, who Gaga had never met, was working on the port and it was his address that had been given to him.

97. JAMIE KNOBLAUCH FAMILY RECIPE

Chicken Liver Pate

This family recipe has been handed down through the
generations from Jamie's Grandfather

Ingredientsl
1 Pound chicken liver
1 onion, diced
5 cloves of Garlic Diced
2 stick celery
1/2 Pound butter cubed
Teaspoon marjoram
Salt and pepper to taste
Tablespoon mustard
1-2 Tablespoon of Brandy or Port (I prefer 2 table spoons
for a richer taste)
2 Tablespoons of Rapeseed oil

Method
Add the Oil to a pot and cook the Garlic, onion, and
Celery on a medium heat for 5-10 min until soft and
translucent
At this point pierce the chicken livers with a sharp knife or
fork, and add to the pan with the veg, Cook for another 5-
10 minutes or so until the livers are almost cooked.

Now add the Port or Brandy, and let it cook off for a
minute or two before adding the Mustard, Marjoram, and
butter.
Once the butter has melted and is bubbling cook for
another 3-4 minutes.
Let cool for 5-10 minutes then Blend using a food
processor or hand blender.
Once blended pass through a sieve to ensure a smooth
consistency, pop it in a jar to cool a bit before putting it in
the fridge to set.

This will last for about a week in the fridge

MARK

JAMES

Opa's Sugar Lab

James and Mark have great stories about their grandfather

Our names are James (9) and Mark (6), we are brothers and live in Cork with our parents. My Mum is German, so we called our Grandfather "Opa" Unfortunately he passed away.He was a very nice and calm Opa, always so excited to see us.

Opa worked in a sugar factory, where he invented things. He invented and developed a machine to make icing sugar stay soft when stored in a warehouse or shop. One of our favourite stories from him is when he used to bring free chocolate and treats home to our mum and her sister to test.

Opa also told us that he did funny tests in his lab, for example "the chewing gum test," which was to see how long strips of chewing gum would stay rigid before bending. We are not sure what it was for, but it sounds like fun! Also, we think we got his passion about anything to do with the sea from him. He lived so far away from the beach in Germany, that coming to Ireland and being so close to the sea was amazing for him. Whenever we are at the beach with our parents, we put our hands into the water to remember Opa. When we grow up, we would like to be Marine Biologists and study about our favourite sea creatures- sea slugs and goblin sharks.

Opa also loved Lighthouses, so here are our pictures

99. ELIZABETH & HER GRANDAD

All about my grandad

Elizabeth's grandad tells her all about the family donkey

The story begins with the donkey coming to the kitchen window to get bread. He would eat the bread and go away. We also used the donkey to bring home turf for the fire.
We also took trips on the donkey up and down the road. Then we would take him home. We would then take off his saddle and then feed him.
I played football on the green with my brothers. We made a bow and arrows with pieces of trees and strings and played with them

100. MELANIE & HER GRANDMOTHER

Grandma's Fright

Melanie Looks Like Her Grandma

Although my grandmother had three daughters and three granddaughters, I was the only granddaughter who resembled her. Looking at photos of my grandma and myself at different ages, it can be hard to tell us apart. When my aunt digitised thousands of family photos, the facial recognition software she used to sort them would routinely mistake me for my grandma and vice versa!

I grew up only a few blocks away from my grandma and would often sleep over at her house on Friday nights. One night I fell asleep in her bed while she was still downstairs chatting with the rest of my family. Hours later, deep in sleep, I was woken suddenly by a scream! I sat up in bed and my grandma was standing there laughing. She said

I walked in here and saw you sleeping and thought it was ME in the bed!

101. EMER & HER GRANDMOTHER

**Emer's Golfing Grandmother - Emer's grandmother
was a pioneer for Lady's Golf**

Maureen took up golf in 1982 at age of 54. She was a stay-
at-home mother of 7, who worked tirelessly keeping
students and volunteering with meals on wheels. Up to
then her interest in sport was as a spectator. She loved golf
from the beginning. One of the things that annoyed her
though was that Ladies could not be full members of the
club. They could only be Associate members which meant
Male members had priority on first tee and Ladies were
restricted in when they could play.

She got involved in Committees and pushed for more
equality for Ladies. She became Lady Captain in 1995 and
was the First Lady Captain to request a blazer with club
crest on it, up to then the Male Captain and President who
had to be a man wore blazers. She also instated a Drive in
for the Lady Captain, up to then only the Male Captain
and President had a Drive in.

In the late 1990s she was part of a committee involved in
getting equality for ladies in golf, this was spearheaded by
the Irish Ladies Golf Union. After a lot of hard work
Ladies were offered full membership in 2000. Ladies then
had the option to stay as Associates or take full
membership. She took up full membership even though a
lot of her friends did not as there was an extra cost.
She said I am doing this for the future generation my
granddaughters in particular so that they will be able to
stand on first tee as equals and also have more playing
rights. In 2016 a Lady became President of the club for the
first time and a lady will be President every 3 years from
then on. So Lady golfers have a lot to be thankful to my
grandmother for

102. PILAR & MARIA

My mom was only 10 when it happened. She was born on
May 22nd, 1987. One day in the sunshine, my mom was
outside on her bike, playing with cousins and having fun.
Then it happened! She was going down a hill really fast.
She couldn't control her bike and then BOOM!

She fell off her bike and she broke her two front teeth
(these were her two front adult teeth). She was bawling
crying and for 2 weeks, I think, she could only drink stuff
and not eat food.

Now she has two front teeth that are made out of
porcelain.

Maria shared this story with Pilar

103. KASEY & HER GREAT GRANDAD

The Heroic Woman

One beautiful morning my great grandad was out for a long walk. He saw a woman, a child and a dog were walking down a boreen. There was also a big fat cow and a tiny calf.

The big fat cow was scared that the dog was going to kill the calf. So then the big fat cow, who looked like a bull, attacked the woman so the dog would run away and not come back. The woman threw the child up in the big green ditch in order to save the small child's life.

The child survived but unfortunately the woman did not. My great grandad saw all this happen and he got scared.

I really like this story because it shows how different the world is now compared to how it was a few years ago. Like how they walked everywhere and had dogs to protect them.

Kasey's great grandad shared this story with her

104. CHLOE & KAREN

Long ago when it was Hallowe'en my mom had no costume so my mom dressed up as a bin bag with a mask. When people saw her they were surprised. They laughed and said, "very good".

When she went to school people laughed but loads of people took a picture. Everybody loved it.

My mom lived in Carrigaline. My nana and granda still live there now.

Karen shared this story with Chloe

105. MAEVE, NANA & JERRY

My nana's name is Dolores. She was born in 1936.

Things that happened in 1936:

Aer Lingus made its first flight to Bristol. Nana has two sisters in Bristol. Their names are Anne and Brenda.

King George V (the fifth) died.

World War 2 was about to start.

My nana and grandad had 8 children. They have 14 grandchildren and they have 4 great grandchildren and another one on the way!

There are 8 children in my dad's family, he always had someone to play with! They always had such fun.

One day they were playing hide and go seek. My dad was hiding. Before he went into his hiding spot, which was the hotpress, he opened his bedroom window. He did it so everyone would think he was hiding outside. They were looking for him for ages. They were looking and getting worried! They came back to check inside. He jumped out and scared them!

Nana & Jerry shared this story with Maeve

106. LILY & NANA

The Blue Budgie

My nana was on a walk with her dad. He heard something in a bush. He put his hand into the bush and there was a blue budgie. They brought the budgie home.

My nana's dad got out a matchstick. He strapped the matchstick to the budgie and fixed the budgie's wing with it. Then he got out a cage from their bird shed. They had a lot of birds. And then he put the budgie in it.

Then the next day they went to the garden and they let the budgie go.

I like this story because it is about animals and my great grandad helped a budgie.

The End.

Nana shared this story with Lily

107. TULISA, WINNIEFRED & MARY

Growing up in a Wagon

When my nanny was a young girl she was brought up in a wagon with her brothers and sisters. They used to cook their food on a fire that my great grandad used to light every day.

My nanny used to drive a blue van. She didn't like driving cars. She used to collect loads of stuff and go to the car-boot sale every Sunday. She would bring her pet dog, Spike, with her.

My life now is very different compared to my nanny's life long ago! We cook our food in an oven and I live in a house now. But we still have my other nanny's blue van and it is very special.

Winniefred and Mary shared this story with Tulisa

108. SARAH & SONY

It was a beautiful day. My mom was going to school.
Then she met the stray dog gang (a pack of stray dogs).
She said hi to them and she left and hopped on the school
bus and off she went.

A few hours later around 3 o'clock she came back from
school and saw the stray dogs and quickly walked away.
She was too kind to do that so she went in, did her
homework and ate her lunch.

After, she went to the dogs to give the chicken leftovers
(to the dogs). She put healing powder on the dogs so she
was happy helping the dogs until she saw her mom. She
quickly ran inside.

Sony shared this story with Sarah

109. MARTA & HER MOM

My Mom's First Day of School

My mom started school when she was five years old and in her school there was only three rooms. In the school she only had one yard and there were only four teachers in the school.

She had one friend in that school and her name was Julia. My mom really liked school. I liked listening to her talk about her school.

My school is very different. My school definitely has more than three rooms and four teachers.

My mom really liked her principal when she was in school. She really liked her because she was always nice to the children. I am just like my mom because I really like my principal too.

My mom went to school in Romania. Schools in Romania were very different to schools in Ireland. They had lots of different subjects in school and learned lots of different things. I go to school in Ireland. I like listening to my mom when she tells me stories like this. I like learning about how things were different long ago. When she tells me stories I learn lots of new things that I did not know before.

Marta's mom shared this story with her

110. DIRK's FAMILY HISTORY

Tracing My Family History - Dirk Traces His Family History Back 400 Years

About 400 years my family were founding members of the St. Sebastian's Celebrations in my German hometown Lengfurt. These celebrations are a religious tradition. According to oral lore, in 1632 Lengfurt was nearly wiped out by the bubonic plague. Only 5 households did survive at the time.

The surviving members swore an oath to St. Sebastian to celebrate his names day every year if he would spare their lives from the disease. And so we are still celebrating this festival every year. Usually the celebration takes place in the shape of a military parade. The celebrations last for a full weekend, close to the 20th January, which is St. Sebastian's names day.

I am a direct descendant

As I can trace the existence of my family in Lengfurt back to the 15th century: I am convinced that my family was one of those founding families. Every year a number of Herberich representatives are actively celebrating "Sebastiani", and I do take every effort to fly to Germany in January to join in actively.

In the last couple of years - except for the COVID year of 2020 - four Herberich family members have been actively celebrating the tradition. You can find more details about the festival here: https://sebastiani-lengfurt.de --> The Google translation into English is reasonably OK, i.e. understandable. If you look closely you may spot me in one of the pictures! * Please note that there are some inaccuracies in the information that has been passed down through the centuries.

I assume that the tradition does actually date back to 1612, when a very bloody civil war in our area ended. After that war our village was forcefully reformed back from lutheranism to catholicism. My assumptions are based on the records of our local church books. The existing records were started on 6th October 1612 with a gruelling statement at the top of the page:

Peste grassante

When the bubonic plague rampaged through the village. Entry number 7 on that date is recording the death of the wife and the 3 children of Johann Herberich (junior). Johann married for a second time on 10th February 1614. I am a direct descendant of the family that Johann had with his second wife.